Ironing with Sue Lawley

Dear Daphne

Here it is!

I hope you like it

Heaps of love

Pauline x

June 2005

Also by Pauline Prior-Pitt

Waiting Women (1989)
(Revised Edition 1999)

In the Heat of the Moment (1992)

Still Standing in the Plant Pot (1994)

Addresses & Dreams 1997
(Revised Edition 2004)

Waiting Women CD (2003)
Live recording of selected poems

Storm Biscuits (2001)
Poems about the Island of North Uist

Pauline Prior-Pitt

Ironing with Sue Lawley

SPIKE PRESS

Ironing with Sue Lawley
published by SPIKE PRESS in 2005

Publisher: SPIKE PRESS
              112 Broomfield Road, Coventry CV5 6JZ
              Tel: 01876 560360

Distributor: AVANTI BOOKS
              Unit 9, The io Centre, Whittle Way,
              Arlington Business Park,
              Stevenage SG1 2BD
              Tel: 01438 747 000

Printed and bound in Scotland by Highland Printers
13 Henderson Road, Longman North, Inverness IV1 1SP

ISBN 1 872916 34 1

Acknowledgements:
I am grateful to the editors of POETRY SCOTLAND
and SECOND LIGHT where several of these poems
first appeared.

Pauline Prior-Pitt is a freelance writer, performer and after dinner speaker. She now lives with her husband on the Isle of North Uist in the Outer Hebrides but travels to the mainland several times a year to give performances and to see her three children and her two grandsons.

THANKS

Thank you to Daphne Powis for her wisdom and guidance, to Jean Saffell, Charlotte Miller, Barbara Jagger and Robert Prior-Pitt for their constant support and, once again, to Sally McKeown, editor of SPIKE PRESS for always being there.

For Robert, Paul, Charlotte & Adam
with love

CONTENTS

A Woman's Prayer   1
Relaxation Class   2
Today   3
Sometimes a Thought   4
A Shedding of Red   5
At Low Water   6
Seal Pool at Traigh Ear   7
Blue and Gold   8
Finding You   9
Late Storm   10
After the Storm   11
Cluster I   12
Cluster II   13
Stone   14
Getting In   15
The Artist   17
Angus McPhee Exhibition   18
Café at the Edinburgh Gallery of Modern Art   20
Sixty   21
Retired Winter Mornings   22
Getting Up   23
Fog Brain   24
Facing It   25
Hands   26
She Needed to Know   27
Weighing Yourself   28
Like Some Sort of Goddess   30
Visiting Jo Malone   31
Above the Level   33

Birthday Walk	34
Ruby Wedding Dream	35
Ironing with Sue Lawley	37
The Basket	39
Strange Bag Fellows	40
The Visit	41
He Was the One	42
To a Daughter in Waiting	44
Grandchild	45
Grandson Visiting	46
French Exchange in Cahors Market	47
Hot in Cahors	48
One Night	49
Petit Dejeuner Complet	50
Old Arguments	51
Impossible Dream	52
Lost Keys	54
Postcards	56
If He Dies First	57

A WOMAN'S PRAYER

Oh Lord! Grant me
one whole day in the house alone,
a day from before dawn until after sunset,

a day from morning until evening
or from after breakfast until dinner time.
No, no, cancel that, thinking about dinner will ruin the day.

Grant me one whole day to be
master of the house. Not mistress;
master of the house, all day.

Well Lord! It's hard to explain the difference it makes,
the tidiness stays tidy, meals are taken lightly,
but it's more than that.

Alone is separate, spacious.
I may do everything. I may do nothing.
Limitless hours of possibility release the day.

Oh Lord! On second thoughts,
grant me two whole days
in the house alone.

RELAXATION CLASS

After they have tightened every muscle and let go,
relaxed their eyelids and let their tongues hang loose,
the voice invites them to imagine a peaceful place,
suggests strolling along a beach, floating in water.

And she imagines a room where she goes to be alone.
Everywhere is cream and white, lit by light through linen.
There's a low table with a pale ceramic bowl
and a sofa where she nestles with a glass of wine
staring into her own silence.

The voice asks her to stretch away and away now,
to open her eyes when she's ready. There's no hurry.
And she lies there, tasting the wine, keeping her eyes tight shut.

TODAY

Today I'm staying in bed with my book
And when anyone says
Are you going to get up now?
I'll say
No.

And when anyone says
What's for lunch?
I'll say
You decide.

And when anyone says
There's no bread in the bin.
I'll say
That's too bad.

And when anyone says
There aren't any clean cups.
I'll say
What a shame.

And when anyone says
Are you going to get up now?
I'll say
Today, I'm staying in bed with my book.

Tomorrow, I'm going out.

SOMETIMES A THOUGHT

Sometimes a thought
can cause a rush of blood,
an inside blush.
It's not a thought you'd share.

Then someone, somewhere,
lets that thought
fall from her lips without a care
and no one is concerned.

They all agree with her,
and you're relieved to know you're not alone,
and wonder why you thought you were.

A SHEDDING OF RED

From the top of the dunes
the sea looks dark pink
and you can't quite believe a dark pink sea.

Feathery threads of red seaweed;
millions and millions held in suspension
as each wave lifts, lifts and breaks,
breaks into pink champagne.

And left on shore, as the water ebbs
crimson hair patterns the edge,
patterns the edge in a shedding of red.

AT LOW WATER

Watch her hurry down the field in wellingtons,
almost losing them in boggy places.
Watch her slip through the brown painted gate
in the stock fence that keeps sheep in,
and stumble over sharp rocks to the shore,
where bladder wrack is slippery: mud sucks her boots.

Watch her wade the shallow stream,
climb the cockle bank onto soft sand.
Miles of white against blue.
Until she comes to the tidal island
where grass is a soft hair nest
stitched with thrift and purple sea asters.

At the sea's edge, there's a line of rocks
where seals rest beside a deep pool hidden in a sandbank.
You cannot see her slip into the pool
swimming close to the seals,
cannot feel cold sea closing round her,
cannot touch the holy silence at low water.

SEAL POOL AT TRAIGH EAR

The pool is deep enough to dive in,
scoured out against a rock by winter storms.
It's far out in the bay; hidden in a sandbank
even at low tide.

Seals bounce themselves down the rock
when I come close, flop into the tidal water,
pop up to watch. Their brown eyes wonder
if they knew me long ago
                    and I remember tales
of seals bearing the souls of drowned sailors
and feel shy taking off my clothes.

When I slip into the pool, they'll dive deep and away
returning at a safe distance
our heads bobbing to each other as we swim.

BLUE AND GOLD

There was that evening
blue and gold
across the empty bay
me miles out in it
me and the warm rocks
me and the rock pool
me swimming naked
in blue and gold.

FINDING YOU

I did not expect to find you here
although I should have known that you would come,
would find this place when you had ceased to be
and come here knowing I would find it too.

I only find you here on peaceful days,
on silent days of solitude and grace,
when emerald and turquoise seas are still
and St Kilda Island is a distant haze.

Your warmth is in the Marram I brush through.
Clover drifts your scent across the breeze.
Soft dunes embrace me down towards the shore.
Your laugh surfs at the edges of the waves.

LATE STORM (June 17th)

In winter, we accept your prowling wind,
your marching hail across our windows.

We know that out of doors we will be whipped
and lashed, rushed faster than we want to go.

We drive to cliffs where we can stand
and watch in awe as heaving seas

smash boulders onto rocks, and waves as high as blocks of flats
fling pebbles up into the air and crash them at our feet.

In May or early June we still expect you. And we are cautious.

But to come so late this year, to come in summer's bloom
so near the solstice,

when soft green leaves of alders are full open,
goat willows newly planted,

when lovage overflows the sheltering wall,
broad beans reach their height,

when irises fill ditches with their floppy sunshine dresses
and bog cotton trembles on the moor.

To come now in your February mood to strip and smash
and burn our bounty black with salt
is hard for us to bear.

AFTER THE STORM

The shore that yesterday was silver sand
is covered to the brim in kelp

as if beneath the sea a battle raged
and corpses were flung up to expiate

the god of storms, or Neptune seething out of sorts
tore up a thousand, thousand, limbs

to make a wasteland where no man may tread.
They lie in heaps, tangled, broken, dead.

And where the late sun pierces glistening fronds,
the beach shines red.

CLUSTER 1

Not a congregation beach
of pebbles heaped by waves.

Not standing proud, jutting
from the sand, after wind blow.

Just now and then the pebbles cluster
washed together between tides.

CLUSTER II

After the odd lonely cottage
scattered in the landscape

arriving at a cluster
overlapping, intimate, not quite a street,

a congregation of old friends
who grew together hearing the same songs.

STONE

Not just any stone,
abandoned by glaciers, on the headland.

A shelter stone perhaps,
in a land without trees, its huge squat shape
protecting all directions.

It's flat on top,
with sides that might have once been carved.

An altar stone perhaps,
standing just outside the ancient wheelhouse.
Gods need sacrifice in this wild place.

Lichen spreads gold circles.
Vetch and thrift decorate small crevices.

A blessing stone perhaps,
a place to bless each other on those special days.
It could become a blessing stone.

GETTING IN

How the sea grips your ankles in ice
and you have to run back to warm sand.

How it cuts the backs of your knees
so you're not going in, it's too cold to swim
and you wade back out to the shallows.

How it freezes the tops of your thighs,
how you cup water in your hands
to give your arms a warning wash
and you wade back out to the shallows.

How you gasp as inch by inch
it slow-tortures your belly.
How if anyone was making you do this, you would refuse
and you wade back out to the shallows.

How waves slap your waist
and you jump up and down,
wrapping your arms, holding your elbows.
How you stand still

waiting for the moment to plunge.
How you scream as the sea bites
the back of your neck
and you have to swim fast to keep warm.

How it's lovely once you're in
letting the cold seep into you,
lifting in emerald waves,
floating, weightless as prayer.

How when you wade back out
the shallows are warm as bathwater.

THE ARTIST

Low winter light has spread
a tapestry across the moor
and water ribbons cut in peat
reflect the sky, a deeper shade
of oiled aquamarine.

He gathers gold beside the road
drags up dark heather roots
and stepping like a goblin
picks bog grass stalks of crimson
to add to his collection.

Inside his room, without the sun on fire
bright colours fade, like pebbles
taken once as jewels from a pool.
But with what he has, he will remember
and capture a watercolour.

ANGUS McPHEE EXHIBITION
gentleman, weaver of grass, South Uist

A gentle man,
harnessing his power
into rough rope
weaving grass garments
for his own reasons.

Pulling at straws in the wind
wearing his grass hat
a woven handkerchief
peeking from his top pocket.

Holding his tongue
weaving words only
into grass vestments
for a green god,
now faded to russet.

Outsize,
to match his aura perhaps,
huge shirts, trousers, boots,
sandals of beach leaves,
a sower's pouch,
and a harness for a pony,

hang on white-washed gallery walls.
His private collection.

Sorrow follows us round
as we marvel at his obsession.
Twist, stroke, plait,
weave, seam, thread,
thread through,
thread through.

CAFÉ AT THE EDINBURGH GALLERY
OF MODERN ART

"Don't let her take the tea strainer away
I may want a second cup," he says
striding off to find the lavatory
and a baby distressed by the quality of modern art
sobs in her mother's arms.

The landscapes and portraits are by Auerbach.
We marvel at paint spread like set custard,
stand well back hoping to glimpse his subjects,
wonder if Hilda really looked like that.
Was she supposed to be vomiting?

Our chocolate torte is thick rich.
We spoon fat scoops into our mouths,
leave brown landscapes on our plates
but don't attempt portraits.
The waitress removes them without comment.

"Leave the tea strainer for the Earl Grey," I say.
"After so much richness we may need a second cup."

SIXTY

Sixty is now.
Seventy will come sooner.
Eighty might not be over the hill.

RETIRED WINTER MORNINGS

You can get up late for a start,
no setting out in the dark
scraping ice off the car.

You can stay where you are,
lie till it's light, without guilt.
You might have been up
in the night to go to the loo,
might not have slept very well,
although mostly you do.
For eight or nine hours
you sleep straight through.
Anyway, you don't need an excuse.

Tea in bed is no longer an occasional treat,
it's habitual, with biscuits,
and an early morning read
and maybe even a second cup,
before eventually, when thoughts of breakfast
become overwhelmingly tempting,
you begin to think about getting up.

GETTING UP

Washing and dressing
and eating her breakfast
just used to happen.
It was something she did

between waking and working,
something she did
without thinking about it.
She didn't notice.

She's noticing now.
It's a slow motion process
like moving through water,
completely absorbing

observing each action
that needs her attention.
Sitting and staring,
heaving and sighing,

flossing and brushing,
washing and dressing,
forgetting…
losing and finding.
It takes half the morning.

And that's without breakfast!

FOG BRAIN

I can't remember
what you asked just now.

I remember riding
curled like a bud in a leaf
on Dad's cross bar,

remember nasturtiums
on grandma's plates
taste her sticky chocolate cake,

can recite the whole of
"the king asked the queen and the queen asked the dairy maid,
could she have some butter"…
Butter!
Did you ask me to pass the butter?

I can't remember.

FACING IT

The furrows in between my brows are permanent.
They only disappear when I looked shocked,
not just surprised; shocked enough
to make my eyebrows rise at least an inch above my eyes.

The creases round my eyes can no longer be described
as smiling lines. They're always there, so well defined,
as are the lines which crease my lips and make the edges
dip in criss-cross fissures down towards my chin.

And underneath my chin, my neck descends
on two slack ropes towards my breasts.
My breasts. Oh this is most depressing
if anything my breasts are sinking even further than the rest.

HANDS

Young, plump,
pale pink flesh
has shrunk
to freckled
wrinkled
paper skin
where veins
criss-cross
in purple knots.
I stop the blood
then let it flow.

SHE NEEDED TO KNOW

She needed to know
her hair looked nice,
smooth at the back,
not sticking out.
But why did she bother?
She was so old. What did it matter?

She needed to know
her dress was just right.
Brown was her colour,
smarter in navy.
But why did she bother?
She was so old. What did it matter?

She needed to tell
she had once been a beauty,
showing the photo,
so tall and slim, almost a model.
But why did she bother?
She was so old. What did it matter?

It mattered of course,
of course it mattered.
I know that now
holding a mirror
up to a mirror
to make sure my hair
is still smooth at the back.

WEIGHING YOURSELF

Never weigh at night, right?
You'll lie awake
thinking the diet's a mistake.
Then because you can't sleep
you'll creep down to the kitchen for tea
and comfort cake.

Never weigh in the day, OK?
But if you have to,
you're at 'Slimmers Anonymous' say,
before you hop onto the scales
remove earrings, necklace, watch,
bracelet, hanky in your pocket, socks,
and quickly cut your nails.

Always weigh naked, in the morning.
Just a warning,
do it before that first cup of tea
and after you have been to the toilet,
properly.
This is the lightest you are going to be.

If you weigh more than you expect, forget.
Move the scales until you find an uneven bit of floor
and try again. Or
stand on the back edge of the scales.
Unless you find, that in your case,
this makes you weigh even more.

As a last resort,
place the scales beside the bath
or next to a chest of drawers.
As you step gently on the scales,
rest your hand on the top of the bath or chest
and press. Then slowly let the pressure off.

Step off… when you like.
This gives the perfect weight,
the best you can ever expect.
By the way,
if anyone asks about your weight,
look them straight in the eye. And lie.

LIKE SOME SORT OF GODDESS

You thought you had five minutes
but he's by the front door
rattling the car keys,
two bottles under his arm. Hungry.

And this dress is too tight.
It should hang straight.
You cannot breathe in all night
and eat.

What will the others wear?
You would like to go in sexy strappy black,
never get the chance. And high heels
but will they be in T shirts and jeans?

You see yourself in the perfect dress,
a dream dress that doesn't exist.
You can't quite describe it.
It's simple and classic.

It's a dress to turn heads.
It hangs straight from the shoulder.
It makes you look younger,
like some sort of goddess.

You pull on black trousers
slip into your cream silk shirt,
check there's no lipstick on your teeth,
and shout down to tell him to start the car.

VISITING JO MALONE

Just inside the door
is a table set with fragrances
and little paper sticks to spray the fragrance on,
though wrists will give a truer test.

The assistant treats me like a friend,
and I forget girls in department stores,
whose perfect makeup's never flawed,
whose looks tell me I'm far too old.

This 'friend' in Jo Malone's excites me,
asks if I like citrus, woody, light green floral, spicy
and when I can't make up my mind,
invites me to try them all.

A woman joins me at the table.
She's been here before; loves floral.
She sprays *Vintage Gardenia* on our wrists.
The mix with cardamom and myrrh is irresistible.

Now we're confused; too many mingling scents
but then we're given roasted coffee beans to smell.
This aroma clears our nasal palettes.
and like connoisseurs we carry on.

We start again on citrus scents,
fresh limes, and zesty mandarin.
Verbenas of Provence is summer in a bottle.
I love the lemon fragrance on my skin.

The oblong bottle with its silver top
nestles in a pale cream box tied with black ribbon.
The pale cream carrier edged in black is signed JM,
and as I pay, we talk about the pleasure this has been.

No overheated changing rooms.
No mirrors showing excess flesh. No sweat. No stress.
We all agree, compared to buying clothes,
buying fragrance is a breeze at Jo Malone's.

ABOVE THE LEVEL

All afternoon, she heaves stones
in her gravel garden,
from where they lie in shadow
flat along a rock ledge

and stacks them one on one,
to make dynamic shapes of stone on stone,
creating height above the level,
mica on stone reflecting winter light.

Her fine raked gravel is now occupied.
Tall sculptures interrupt the level,
disturb her horizontal surface.

At dusk she lifts off every stone,
heaves them back along the rock ledge,
places them flat, in shadow.

BIRTHDAY WALK

Halfway down the field greylags rise,
flap their wings in celebration, honk their blessings.
And sheep come bleating curiosity.

Seagulls gather just above my head,
screech their greetings, try to warn me off their eggs.
I shout to tell them they will have to share the beach with me.

The sea's miles out in the bay
and the wind rushes me, and my hat, across wet sand,
towards the island, capped just now in thistle stalks and grass.

Nestled in the lee, it's warm, a place to sit and wonder.
It's my 'Will you still need me, will you still feed me?' birthday
and my breakfast tray was set with freesias and champagne.

RUBY WEDDING DREAM

In the middle of her night,
dressed in cotton white pyjamas
and Auntie Mary's fancy garden hat -
the pyjamas are broiderie anglaise
the hat is straw and lined in red.
The pyjamas look delicious
when they're fresh and newly ironed
but crumple into nothing
once they have been slept in -
so in the middle of her night
dressed in cotton white pyjamas
and Auntie Mary's fancy garden hat

she climbed onto her bicycle
and rode off… to her wedding.
Not sure where she was going
she cycled through a village
and noticed in a window
a display of sexy lingerie.
She wasn't wearing underwear
well not under pyjamas
but now it seemed unseemly
to be so barely clad.
She leaned her bike against the window
although a notice said she shouldn't
and entered the establishment
to finger all the lingerie.
She found red silk, lace-trimmed knickers.
She found garters, basques, and brassieres.
Black satin. Plunging necklines.
She was really spoilt for choice.   35

Under piles of lace and satin
she unearthed her wedding dress,
white velvet with white buttons
from the hem up to the neck.

Abandoned on the floor
lay her cotton white pyjamas.
and propped on top lay
Auntie Mary's fancy garden hat.
Fastened were the buttons
from the hem up to her neck
and on her head a veil
with a swansdown coronet.
But when she looked into the mirror
she saw to her distress,
an ancient grey haired woman
wore a young bride's dress.
Abandoned on the floor lay
white velvet and white buttons.
In a bundle lay her veil
with the swansdown coronet.

And dressed in cotton white pyjamas,
knickers, lace trimmed, silk, and red,
she climbed onto her bicycle
and rode back home to bed.

IRONING WITH SUE LAWLEY

The actress chooses Romeo and Juliet.
Prokofiev's music smoothes my sheets
until his dancing knights clash in alarm.
Who ironed Juliet's sheets, the ones they stained
before they spoke of nightingales and larks?

Does Shakespeare mention ironing at all?
It never plays a central role, just off stage left perhaps
a glimpse of servants pressing folds into their masters' ruffs.
Cinderella did her fair share for those ugly sisters
and I expect the dwarfs kept Snow White, white.

White is what I'm ironing just now,
a cotton duvet cover stitched with daisies.
Folded in half the edges never come together,
one side is always wider than the other.
It takes at least three records without creases.

I like it when the guest's someone I know,
well feel as if I know, if you know what I mean:
actors, artists, writers, even politicians.
I hate it if they choose all rock or pop,
love classical or something very modern.

Just nosing round the buttons on his shirt
when Barber's adagio for strings begins.
She chose it to remind her of her mother.
I have to set the iron down to stare,
the longing and the darkness and my own.

Then I remember Alison of course,
whose ironing board was centre stage,
who pressed her anger into shirts all through Act 1.
Did Jimmy feel the anger when he put them on?
Will sadness seep from mine?

If she can take only the one, she's taking Barber
And for her luxury she chooses a vibrator
with a special solar powered battery.
I'd take knickers and a crate of bottled water
but Sue would say that doesn't count as luxury.

I'll need somewhere to lie and read the Bible:
a comfortable, soft embracing place,
a queen size bed, white duvet
stitched with daisies, freshly pressed
by someone off stage left.

THE BASKET

She's weaving a basket choosing gold stems of marram
to wrap round her fingers testing for strength,
weaving the marram in front and behind
adding more layers, keeping hold of the basket.

She's filling her basket with clutter from cupboards,
pulling dresses off hangers and shoes out of boxes,
emptying her drawers and filling her basket.

She's carrying her basket over-full in her arms,
bending over once more to pick up the fallen,
taking her basket down to the sea.

She's tracing along the edge of the tide line,
right foot on the soft sand, left foot in the water.
She's casting her basket to float on the ebb tide.
She's casting her basket to float out to sea.

STRANGE BAG FELLOWS

In a calico bag
with calico handles,
rosemary baked ham,
cut in thick slices,
slips down beside
Ukrainian rye bread
lying next to a cabbage
and two Danish pastries
on top of two books
of New Penguin poets,
Liz, Roger and Sharon,
Vicky, Eavon and Carol Ann,
and the Swiss army pen knife
bought for a nephew.
It's his birthday on Tuesday.

THE VISIT

When my son lives in a house of his own
I will visit him.
I will drop my coat, hat and bags
on the floor,
just inside the door,
and demand to know when tea will be ready.

I will switch on the TV
to full volume,
and lie on the floor in my duvet
with a bowl of shredded wheat
milk to the brim
which, when empty,
I will slide under the settee.

I will shout at him
for tidying away my things,
refuse to sit up to the table
until my programme has finished
and say, it is definitely not my turn
to help with the washing up.

When I arrive,
he welcomes me,
takes my coat,
ushers me into his tidy sitting room,
pours tea into thin china and offers me cake.
We talk like old friends.

HE WAS THE ONE

He was the one
with his hand in iced water
cooling the burn.

He was the one
who found
only one shoe.

He was the one
not wearing a coat;
not even in winter.

He was the one
who was always late,
who knew his teacher didn't like children,

who when he was seven,
said he could manage
without going to school.

He was the one
who stayed in bed,
who wore his dressing gown all day long

who wouldn't be told,
who found out for himself,
who passed his exams in his own time.

He is the one who became the teacher
who knows all about children who won't be told
and he knows how to tell them

what really matters;
how it's the journey that counts,
not arriving too soon.

He is the one who's OK,
about death
being close to arriving.

TO A DAUGHTER IN WAITING

Stronger than butterflies,
inside me a trapped bird
batters its wings against my soft walls.

All day I think of you,
begin a thousand jobs,
stand in the middle of the room
not going left, not going right.

Your blue eyes in the photograph
look deep trust in me.
I have not prepared you for the pain.

GRANDCHILD

Before he's born you can't understand
what the fuss is about. You're not
even bothered about having one.

Friends bore you with incessant chat
about their sleeping patterns, eating patterns,
bowel movements, the funny things they say.

They always have packs of photos
taken from every angle, and you
wonder if they know there's a war on.

And then your own love affair begins.
He is exceptionally beautiful of course
everyone will want to see the photographs,

will want to listen when you tell them
all the funny things he does, how well he sleeps
how very, very special he is.

And your dear grandmother friends
who know all about this obsessive love
indulge you, agree he is exceptionally beautiful.

And you discover that their incessant chat
about their grandchildren is compelling
and the war can wait.

GRANDSON VISITING

We'll fill his bucket to the brim with gravel,
struggle up worn steps to pour it onto rocks
and listen to the crunching as it falls.

We'll struggle down the steps
to fill his bucket to the brim once more
and pour it on the rocks again.

And do this ten times over
each time delighting in the crunch.

We'll go inside the shed
and hold the screwdriver
like Grandpa does, and put it back,

hold it again, and put it back,
and hold the hammer again and again.

We'll stand at the edge of the sea
throwing pebbles into waves,
and stretch our pockets wet with shells.

And this time when he comes,
there will be lambs.

FRENCH EXCHANGE IN CAHORS MARKET

An old woman, thin as a bird,
caught her shopping trolley on my foot
near to a stall with a thousand lettuces.

"Pardon Madame," she said and gripped my arm,
"Vous etes en vacances?"
"Mais oui." I said, "Je suis anglaise."

"Et je suis Belgue, but during the war
my family sought refuge in Cahors.
Now I am eighty-eight,

too old to carry my basket to the market.
I have nine children."
"I have three." I said, "and deux plus petits."

"Oh! Plus petits, I have twenty three."
Vingt trios, I think she said, "Vingt trios."
I showed her with my eyes, I was impressed.

She loosed my arm, and pushed her trolley
on towards the cheese. "Bon journée, Madame."
"Merci Madame," I said, "Merci," and wandered on.

HOT IN CAHORS

Tall shuttered houses
in narrow medieval streets
shade them as they drift in the heat
from cool drink to cool drink.

In the cathedral, they walk barefoot
on stone flags, curl their hands round brass
press their faces against marble, rest
in the damp crypt,

where a painting of Jesus
washing his disciples' feet
is lit by faint light.

ONE NIGHT

One night they ran right across town
in a thunderstorm
drenched by warm rain, laughing.
Hotel staff came to their room
and took away their clothes to dry.
Elderly guests from Spain
were heard to say,
they are drowned like rats,
they are laughing,
and they are English.
At breakfast everyone smiled.

"PETIT DEJEUNER COMPLET"

"petit dejeuner complet"
was complete enough
fresh croissants, pains au chocolat,
viennoises, brioche,
with raspberry jam, home made, and apricot
and coffee in enormous cups.

OLD ARGUMENTS

Something new strikes the match
but their blaze is always the same.

Raked over coals finding old sparks
smouldering just below their tolerance

burst into flame. And burn
wounds too deep for the thickest bandage.

Too scorched to settle anywhere,
lips so charred they dare not speak,

they tramp the shore. Try to fit their steps together.
Their hands just alight in their pockets.

IMPOSSIBLE DREAM

She was trying to sleep, was almost falling off,
when from his snoring mouth he shouted, 'frog,'
which made her laugh. Then 'put more wax on it,'
he said and slumbered on.

She thought at once how impossible it would be;
frogs are such slippery creatures.
Was the frog made of wood, in need of polishing
and whose frog exactly?

Perhaps 'frog' was an insult he called out
as he left one room, and, in the way of dreams,
fell below stairs and was expected
to bring up the shine on an old bookcase.

Of course, the two utterances could be years apart in a dream.
One moment he's with David Attenborough
identifying amphibians,

the next he's pouring wax for a seal on an important document,
a death warrant: Anne Boleyn's, Sir Thomas More's.
Religion has a lot to answer for. If he calls Henry VIII a frog
he'll live to regret it, or maybe not.

He sounded disgruntled when he shouted 'frog'.
Was he miming his favourite animal at a party
and no one guessed and he had to tell them?

Perhaps he kissed a frog,
who promised to turn into a princess
if he put more wax on his moustache

and he rushed home,
commanded his servant to put more wax on
but by the time he got back she'd hopped off,
and he was cross.

She'll never know.
Next morning he couldn't remember a thing.
But sometimes, when he's being impossible, she says to him,
'Oh go and put some more wax on your frog.'

LOST KEYS

He is beside himself with rage.
You hear him, beside himself.
His familiar words.
"Where are they?
Where the Hell are they?"

And then he is beside you
and you must stop, shaving your legs,
solving the problems of the third world,
stop, even in mid-stream,
to look for his keys.

Should you try to escape this time,
smash your way through the double glazing
screaming, he's lost his keys,
his keys, lost again?
Instead you use your quiet voice to question him.

Has he looked carefully in all his pockets.
This annoys him for some reason
and for some reason which has never been discussed
or agreed between you, he is allowed to scream,
"Of course I've looked in all my pockets."

You don't move, don't join in the frantic lifting,
the looking behind, the 'can't believe they're not here' routine
although you can't resist asking if they're on the hook
where they're supposed to be, next to yours,
which, of course they're not.

You ask: Shelf by the door? No.
By the phone? No. The drawer? No.
In the little basket on the cupboard,
which he drops things into?
(coins, screws, sun glasses, vouchers, nail clippers) No.

Where had he been?
It can only have been yesterday.
What was he wearing when he had them last:
black coat, jacket, anorak, gardening anorak, Mac?
He looked there first of course. "Ah!"

Trousers, which trousers yesterday?
He races upstairs.
Only now do you move, towards his pockets.
"Found them!" you call. "In the pocket of your Mac.
It was raining yesterday."

POSTCARDS

She grumbles that he never writes
letters or cards to their children, family and friends.
Not even to his closest friend, preferring her to write them all.

But today in Chartres, with café au lait for him,
du thé for her, and a perfect millefeuille to share,
he says he would prefer to write all the postcards himself.
Insists on writing to all their shared relationships,
leaving a small space for her to add her name.

But he's not writing what she wants to say.
He's telling them where they're going tomorrow.
She would write about yesterday and earlier today.

He hasn't mentioned the cathedral, how holy it is,
how it's like entering a hushed womb
where light seeps in through stained glass jewels, so dark, so blue,
how they lit candles, even though they don't believe,
how they found a labyrinth set into the nave.

She would mention the cathedral,
would end by saying, "See you when we get back."
She sips her tea watching him. Doesn't offer to lick the stamps.

IF HE DIES FIRST
(for Robert who suggested the idea)

I'll paint all the doors white,
get up as late as I like
and spend the morning in my dressing gown.

I won't bother much about meals,
may not eat breakfast at all
and have egg on toast for dinner.

I'll read in bed for hours,
watch all my favourite programmes,
and hang the large mirror in the sitting room.

I'll lay cream carpets in the upstairs rooms, decorate
our bedroom in pale sand with palest blue grey wood,
and keep the table by the window for one perfect bowl.

I'll turn his workroom into an extra space for guests,
change his shed into a place for me to mess in,
and his green house will become my garden room.

I'll invite my women friends to long intimate lunches,
go for walks beside the sea on summer nights,
and buy a Landrover to drive to hidden beaches.

Oh Hell,
tomorrow I shall buy white paint.